Home Run Heroes

Mark McGwire & Sammy Sosa

BY

MARK STEWART AND **MIKE KENNEDY**

M

THE MILLBROOK PRESS
BROOKFIELD, CONNECTICUT

Produced by
BITTERSWEET PUBLISHING—John Sammis, President
and TEAM STEWART, INC.

Series Design and Electronic Page Makeup by
JAFFE ENTERPRISES—Ron Jaffe

Researched and Edited by
Mariah Morgan

All photos courtesy AP/ Wide World Photos, Inc. except the following:
University of Southern California—Page 13
Texas Rangers Baseball Club—Pages 19, 24
Vesely Photography—Pages 25, 36

The following images are from the collection of Team Stewart:
Newsweek, Inc.—Page 4 (1998)
Pacific Trading Cards, Inc —Page 39 (1988)
Topps Chewing Gum, Inc —Page 10 (1988)
Fleer Corporation—Page 10 (1986, 1987)
All-America Baseball, Inc.—Page 12 (1982)
Baseball America, Inc.—Page 14 (1984)
Statabase, Inc.—Page 21 (1987)
Leaf-Donruss—Page 10 (1985), Page 22 (1988), Page 34 (1992)
Topps Chewing Gum, Inc.—Page 28 (1987)
Rawlings Sporting Goods, Inc.—Page 39 (1955)
American Playing Cards—Page 48 (1950)
Sport Magazine/Macfadden–Bartell Corporation—Page 48 (1962)

Printed in the United States of America

Published by
The Millbrook Press, Inc.
2 Old New Milford Road
Brookfield, Connecticut 06804

Library of Congress Cataloging-in-Publication Data

Stewart, Mark.
Home run heroes : McGwire and Sosa / by Mark Stewart and Mike Kennedy.
    p.   cm.
Includes index.
Summary: Presents the lives, on and off the baseball field, of two athletes whose battle for
the home run record dominated sports headlines in 1998.
    ISBN 0-7613-1559-4 (lib. bdg.). —ISBN 0-7613-1045-2 (pbk.)
    1. McGwire, Mark, 1963–   —Juvenile literature. 2.Sosa, Sammy, 1968–   —Juvenile
literature 3. Baseball players—Dominican Republic—Biography—Juvenile literature.
[1. McGwire, Mark, 1963– . 2. Sosa, Sammy, 1968–   . 3. Baseball players.] I. Kennedy,
Mike. II. Title.   III. Title: McGwire and Sosa.
GV865.A1S84   1999
796.357'092'273—dc21
[B]   98-50292
                                                                                              CIP
                                                                                              AC

        pbk: 1 3 5 7 9 10 8 6 4 2
        lib: 1 3 5 7 9 10 8 6 4 2

Contents

THE SWISSAIR TRAGEDY · MELTDOWN IN THE MARKETS

Newsweek

September 14, 1998 : $2.95 US

Awesome!

Sluggers Sammy Sosa and Mark McGwire

Sammy and Mark leapt off the sports pages and onto the covers of national magazines such as NEWSWEEK. Their home run duel was truly Awesome!

The 1998 baseball season will
forever be remembered as the time when
two amazing players, Mark McGwire of the St.
Louis Cardinals and Sammy Sosa of the Chicago Cubs,
engaged in the most high-powered home run duel in history.
Thanks to the legions of sportswriters and television crews
reporting their every move and utterance, the public was exposed
to waves of information about these stars. Yet, as the season drew to
its thrilling climax, it became increasingly clear that there was much
that fans did *not* know about Mark and Sammy—their lives were laid
out before us in bullet-point form, with little to connect the dots. To
understand the two athletes who dominated the sports headlines in
1998—and truly appreciate what they accomplished—you must
first "rewind" their highlight reels. This book pieces
together the lives of Mark McGwire and Sammy Sosa,
both on and off the field, as they converged on
their appointment with baseball history.

Swinging *Away*

How different would the summer of 1998 have been had Mark McGwire been competing on the pro golf tour instead of on major league baseball diamonds? This notion is not as far-fetched as it might seem. For most of Mark's childhood, in fact, his first love *was* golf. He was swinging a club soon after he took his first steps, and was caddying for his dad when he was five. Soon Mark was hitting the ball straighter and longer than just about any other boy his age.

Baseball did not really come into Mark's life until he was eight. Except for an occasional Wiffle ball game in the cul-de-sac in front of his home, he had little exposure to the sport. But at the urging of a friend, Mark joined a youth league in his hometown of Claremont, California. Mark had a very strong arm, so the team's coach played him at pitcher and shortstop. Mark's hitting was only fair at first, mostly because he was nearsighted. Once he was fitted with glasses, he became the league's most fearsome slugger. Mark moved up to Little League two summers later, and smashed a home run in his first time at bat. As a starting pitcher, he did not lose a game in three seasons.

In any other family, Mark would have been the celebrity. But in the McGwire home, he blended right in. His parents, John and Ginger, were

Mark has been in the baseball spotlight since he hit a home run in his first Little League at bat.

Mark greets the crowd after winning the 1989 World Series. Ten years earlier he quit baseball to take up golf.

both sports enthusiasts. Mark's brothers—Mike, Bobby, Dan, and "J.J."—were all terrific athletes. John and Bobby were big soccer players, Dan was the best quarterback in the area, and J.J. was good at just about every sport he tried, especially football. Because of his size, Mark thought about playing football, too. But in the end, he could not see the sense in practicing five evenings a week just to play one game. Instead, he played soccer. Regardless of the game Mark was playing (and at one time or another he played them all), he brought to it patience, intelligence, and a remarkable work ethic.

By the time Mark enrolled in Damien High School, he was good enough at baseball and golf to be a star in either. The problem was that both were "spring" sports. Mark knew he had to choose one and devote himself to it, or he would not realize his potential. He went to the Damien baseball coach, Tom Carroll, and informed him that he had made his decision: golf.

And that is why Mark McGwire, future home run king, did not pick up a baseball bat during the spring and summer of 1979. By the time he began his junior year at Damien, he had brought his golf handicap down to four, a remarkable number for a fifteen-year-old. Given his physical and mental makeup—and the fact that you can play golf twelve months a year in southern California—there was every reason to believe that he would continue getting better.

Good Stick,
No Leather

In the spring and summer of 1979, playing golf was the farthest thing from ten-year-old Sammy Sosa's mind. He was thinking about how nice it would be just to own a baseball glove. Born in the baseball-mad city of San Pedro de Marcoris, Sammy was already gaining recognition as one of the best young ball players in the Dominican Republic. But money had been tight in the Sosa home since his father, Juan, had died suddenly in 1976 of a brain aneurysm. Any money Sammy made shining shoes, washing cars, or selling fruit went right to his mother, who struggled to make ends meet for her six children and pay the rent on their tiny apartment. Luxuries like gloves, bats, and baseball spikes were just not part of the picture.

Sammy first discovered baseball at the age of five, thanks to his brother, Luis, who took him to a Little League game. Like many boys his age in San Pedro, Sammy spent every free moment playing ball. The Dominican Republic had sent several players to the major leagues, including Rico Carty, Cesar Geronimo, Cesar Cedeno, Joaquin Andujar, and the famous Alou brothers, Felipe, Mateo, and Jesus. The most famous of all was pitcher Juan Marichal. The best young players in San Pedro when Sammy was

Sammy began playing baseball in the streets of San Pedro de Marcoris when he was five. He did not play for an organized team until he was fourteen.

growing up were teenagers George Bell, Juan Samuel, Tony Fernandez, and Julio Franco, each of whom would go on to star in the major leagues. Pedro Guerrero, a third baseman, had signed a contract with the Los Angeles Dodgers. Though still a minor leaguer, he returned each winter to a hero's welcome.

Already familiar with the hard realities of life, Sammy sensed that his family's best chance for survival might come from his considerable skills as a baseball player. Adults often told him that he looked as good or better than players who had been signed by professional teams, and that encouraged him to keep getting better. The natural gifts that enabled Sammy to star in baseball—quick hands, strong arms and shoulders, and great speed—also served him well in the boxing ring. Like young Mark McGwire, Sammy probably had the talent to star in more than one sport. And just as Mark had had to choose, Sammy was compelled to pick one and forget the other. In Sammy's case, it was his brother, Juan, who urged him to make up his mind.

Juan believed Sammy had a much better chance to make it as a baseball player. A growing number of major league scouts were coming to San Pedro to watch the kids play. They would take notes, make suggestions, and sometimes return with contracts in their pockets. The

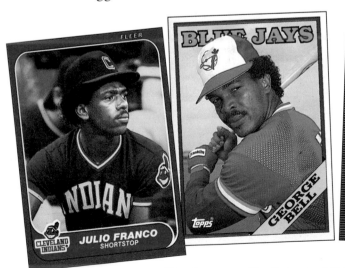
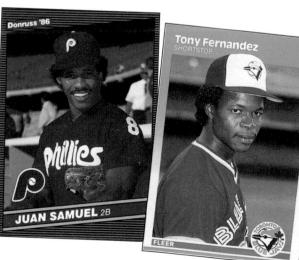

Stardom was "in the cards" for these four Dominicans, who were just a few years older than Sammy.

odds were against making it all the way to the majors, but the bonus money for signing (typically $2,000 to $5,000) could lift a family like the Sosas out of poverty and give them a chance at a better life.

From that moment on, Sammy devoted himself to baseball. Whenever he found a game he tried to get into it, even if adults were playing. If he could not borrow a glove, he played bare-handed. When he could not find a game, he would swing a tree limb at a ball made of wadded-up rags or socks. To develop his legs, Sammy ran barefoot on the beach, moving from harder to softer sand in order to intensify his workout.

In 1981, Sammy caught the eye of Bill Chase. A Florida businessman, Chase owned a manufacturing plant in the Dominican Republic. He noticed how hard Sammy played, and how seriously he took the game. Though hardly an expert, Chase thought that from somewhere inside that skinny, untrained baseball body a star might one day emerge. He gave Sammy his first baseball glove, and told him he looked like the kind of player who could go places. Sammy responded to this unexpected gesture the only way he knew how: by training twice as much and playing twice as hard. Soon it was Sammy's name the scouts were scribbling in their notepads.

Another person who helped Sammy was Hector Peguero, a young man dedicated to helping the kids of San Pedro develop their baseball potential. Peguero taught baseball to children all day long. Those who had a few coins paid him, but most did not. About a year after Bill Chase gave Sammy his first glove, Peguero gave him his first real instruction. In fact, he made Sammy his special project, teaching him how to focus his concentration and working endless hours to tame his boundless energy and his wild swing. When the weather was bad, the two would go indoors, where Peguero further refined Sammy's stroke by making him hit dried corn kernels and bottle caps. In the end, Peguero's greatest contribution to Sammy's development was that he made him feel proud—proud of who he was, what he could do, and where his skills might one day take him. "Everything Hector did took me to another level," Sammy remembers.

Golden *Boy*

A funny thing happened to Mark McGwire on the way to becoming a professional golfer. Making pressure shots and eliciting *oohs* and *aahs* from tournament galleries just did not do it for him. In 1980 the boy everyone had taken to calling "Tree" switched sports again, returning to baseball.

Mark, who now stood 6 feet 5 inches and weighed nearly 200 pounds, picked up right where he left off. He could hit balls a mile, and when he burned his fastball over the plate, the catcher's mitt made a loud popping sound. Mark quickly became the star of the Damien High team, and established himself as one of the country's best American Legion players that summer. During a tournament in Wyoming, he pitched a no-hitter in the championship game.

By Mark's senior season, most scouts in California—both college and pro—had heard of him. He hit .359 with 5 home runs, and fashioned a 5–3 record with a 1.90 ERA. Everyone who saw Mark had a different opinion of how good he would be, and whether he would make a better hitter or pitcher. Pitching coach Marcel Lachemann of the University of Southern California took a special interest in Mark. He saw a young man who had control of both his pitches and his emotions, and could throw

In 1982, ALL AMERICA BASEBALL NEWS ran this blurb on USC's new "hotshot" hurler, Mark "McGuire"!

John Wallace (drafted by Atlanta) will play center field, while Craig Stevenson (drafted by San Francisco) will move in at shortstop, replacing departed All-American Dan Davidsmeier.

Dedeaux also landed two hotshot young pitching prospects, in Sid Akins, the Los Angeles City High School Player of the Year, and **Mark McGuire**, Montreal's 8th draft pick.

the ball 85 to 90 miles per hour. USC offered Mark a scholarship and he accepted.

The next morning Mark woke up with terrible stomach pains. By the day's end he was in the hospital, having his appendix removed and starting treatment for mononucleosis. By the time he recovered, the American Legion season was under way, and there was no sense in trying to get back into shape to pitch. Instead, Mark spent the summer playing first base. He hit .415 with 14 home runs and 53 RBIs, leading Claremont to the state playoffs. That June, Mark was drafted by the Montreal Expos. They offered him $8,500 to turn pro and he refused. Compared to a free college education and a chance to play for USC's legendary head coach, Rod Dedeaux, Montreal's offer seemed ridiculous. Later on, Mark admitted that had the Expos made him a better offer, he would have passed up college and signed with the team.

Mark's first year at USC was one of adjustments—finding his way around a huge campus, dealing with the pressure of joining a

Mark's big swing produced 55 home runs in three seasons with USC.

BaseBall america's
1984 All-America Team

C—JOHN MARZANO
Temple

1B—MARK McGWIRE
Southern California

2B—BOB RALSTON
Arizona

3B—DAVID DENNY
Texas

SS—CORY SNYDER
Brigham Young

OF—ODDIBE McDOWELL
Arizona State

OF—CHRIS GWYNN
San Diego State

OF—RAFAEL PALMEIRO
Mississippi State

DH—PETE INCAVIGLIA
Oklahoma State

P—JOHN HOOVER
Fresno State

P—SCOTT BANKHEAD
North Carolina

P—GREG SWINDELL
Texas

P—SCOTT WRIGHT
Cal State Fullerton

Mark was in good company on BASEBALL AMERICA's All-America Team, with future major league starters Cory Snyder, Oddibe McDowell, Rafel Palmeiro, Pete Incaviglia, Scott Bankhead, and Greg Swindell.

great college team, and trying to hit Division-I pitching. Despite a .200 batting average and just three home runs, Mark never lost his drive to improve. That summer, at the suggestion of Dedeaux and hitting instructor Ron Vaughn, Mark played baseball in Alaska. They not only wanted him to concentrate on hitting, they wanted him to spend a few months away from home. USC was only an hour away from Claremont, and the coaches felt that at times Mark was distracted living so close to home.

At first, Mark was miserable and homesick. His manager that summer in Anchorage, Jim Dietz, recalls Mark standing in the outfield before one game with tears streaming down his face. But as the summer progressed, he realized that playing baseball for a living (which he dearly wanted to do) meant living away from home. He pulled

> *"Well, life is really just a bunch of adjustments, isn't it?"*
>
> —MARK McGWIRE

himself together, played great baseball, and led his team to the finals of the National Baseball Congress tournament.

Upon his return to USC, Mark informed coach Dedeaux that he wanted to become the team's regular first baseman. Knowing he could not devote himself fully to hitting if he continued to pitch, Mark asked if he could be relieved of his hurling duties. Dedeaux grudgingly agreed to the experiment, using Mark only in emergencies.

After a slow start, Mark went on a tear. With a couple of weeks to go in the season, he had already equaled the school record of 17 homers. Hitting number eighteen, however, proved a lot more difficult than he anticipated. For seven games, all Mark could think about was breaking the record, and for seven games he never came close. Finally, when he put the record out of his mind, he hit two homers to finish at 19. It was a lesson he would remember many years later.

Over the next fourteen months, Mark gained recognition as one of the most exciting young hitters in the country. During the summer of 1983, he joined a team of college stars that toured the world. He clouted six homers during the Pan Am Games, and helped Team USA reach the finals against Cuba at the International Cup. Returning to USC for his junior year, Mark was just ten home runs shy of the school's career record of 32. He not only broke the record, he hit 32 in one *season*! That also gave him the NCAA record for career home runs.

In the 1984 major league draft, the Oakland A's made Mark their first selection. After spending another whirlwind summer with Team USA— and competing in the Olympics—Mark signed his first pro contract. He also married his fiancée, Kathy, that year. Everything was going perfectly. Mark was happy, he had money in the bank, and was officially a pro baseball player. He was on his way.

Big Deals &
Value Meals

In 1984, Sammy Sosa thought he was on his way, too. He had just agreed to a contract with the Philadelphia Phillies, the same club with which local stars Bell, Franco, and Samuel (all of whom were now in the majors) had originally signed. Sammy, who was just fifteen, told the Philadelphia scout that he was sixteen—the minimum age at which a prospect can be signed. When the paperwork got to the league office and Sammy's true age was discovered, the contract was voided. He had to wait a little longer before he could cash his first professional paycheck.

After Sammy turned sixteen, the Texas Rangers and Toronto Blue Jays gave him tryouts. The Blue Jays had the inside track by virtue of their reputation for developing Dominicans. The Rangers, on the other hand, did not have a single Hispanic player on their major league roster. Both teams saw the same strengths and weaknesses in Sammy—his swing was a mess and he lacked many of the fundamentals that come with basic coaching—and it worried them that he had not played an inning of actual organized baseball until he was fourteen. Still, there was something about the way the ball rocketed off his bat, and in the field the kid looked like a real player. Texas became the front-runner for Sammy's services when scout Omar Minaya came into the picture. Sammy's mother trusted Minaya and admired his easy manner. In July of 1985, he offered Sammy $3,500 to sign with the Rangers. Sammy agreed to the deal, and gave almost all of the money to his mother. He blew the rest on his first "luxury" vehicle: a new bicycle.

> "He was the kind of person who would ask me for two dollars, then always give one of them to some poor kid who needed it."
>
> —OMAR MINAYA

Sammy played that winter in San Pedro, then reported to the Rangers' rookie-level team in Port Charlotte, Florida, for the 1986 season. Major league teams sign dozens of teenage prospects from Spanish-speaking countries each year, knowing full well that only a handful will survive the first couple of seasons. Adjusting to a new country and a new language without the support of friends and family takes a heavy toll on these players, the vast majority of whom end up right back where they started. Sammy understood what was at stake, and vowed to be one of the kids who made it.

> "We were young guys, and we knew we could play this game...after we got there we realized we had to go out there every day, work on our hitting, and take fly balls every day."
>
> —SAMMY SOSA

Sammy's upbeat attitude helped him through some lonely times in the major leagues

Juan Gonzalez befriended Sammy in 1986 and the two young stars rose quickly through the farm system.

Fortunately, he made a friend on the team his first year who thought the same way. His name was Juan Gonzalez, and he was even skinnier and more frightened than Sammy. The two usually ate together (almost always at fast-food restaurants, where they could simply point to the meal they wanted) and spent hours talking about what it would take to make it to the majors. That first season, Sammy played in 61 games and led the Gulf Coast League in doubles and total bases. Juan led all players in at bats. Looking back, both men credit their manager, Rudy Jamarillo, with helping them get to the next level. He worked them hard; when they complained, he told them that the only way to make the major leagues was to develop a major-league work ethic.

Sammy and Juan spent each of the next two seasons together, as they progressed through the Texas Ranger farm system. At the start of the 1989 campaign, the two moved up to the Class-AA Tulsa Drillers. There Sammy hit for average and power, and tore it up on the bases. After 66 games, a most surprising call came to manager Tommy Thompson. The Rangers, in the heat of a pennant race, had decided to promote Sammy to the majors.

In 1988, Sammy and Juan dreamed about making it to the majors. A decade later, they would share the stage as baseball's Most Valuable Players.

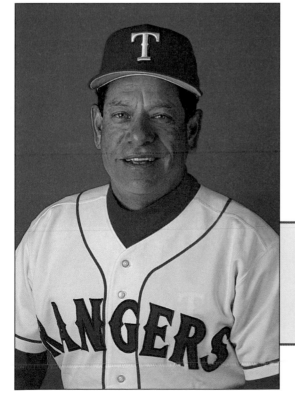

"In a sense, I was real hard on them. I remember Sammy Sosa telling me one time, 'You're worse than the sun because you're like the devil.'"

—RUDY JAMARILLO

Roller
Coaster

The Oakland A's could not believe that Mark McGwire's name was still on the board when it came time for them to make their selection in the 1984 draft. Most teams had Mark listed as their top power prospect, and everyone agreed he would make it to the majors quickly. The reason he slipped down (to 10th) was that the Mets—owners of the first overall pick in the draft—had contacted John McGwire and pressured him into making a deal *before* they actually selected Mark. When he would not, the Mets feared Mark was planning to return for his senior year at USC. That apparently scared off other teams, too.

Nothing, however, was as frightening as what Mark did to minor league pitching. In 1985, his first full year as a pro, he tied for the most home runs and RBIs in the Class-A California League. He also learned a new position, third base, and led the league in assists. The following season, Mark started at Class-AA Huntsville and earned a quick promotion to Oakland's Class-AAA club in Tacoma. Between the two teams, he hit 23 homers and knocked in 112 runs in 133 games. When the minor league

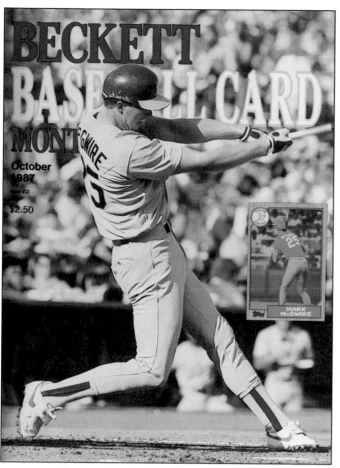

Having the hottest rookie card in the hobby earned Mark a BECKETT'S cover in October of 1987.

season concluded, he was called up to join the A's for the final month of the 1986 campaign. The plan for 1987 was to let Mark and fellow prospect Rob Nelson battle it out for the first base job, with the two rookies eventually forming a powerful righty-lefty platoon.

Mark rendered this plan obsolete the following spring, when he won the job outright. It took him just a few weeks to get the measure of major league pitching, and then he started blasting balls out of the park. In May alone, he hit 15—just one shy of the all-time record for the month. This touched off speculation that he might make a run at Roger Maris's single-season standard of 61. At the very least, it seemed, he would eclipse the rookie record of 38.

For the first time in his life, Mark found himself in the middle of a media circus. Everywhere the A's played, twenty or thirty reporters would crowd around his locker, even if he had just gone 0 for 5. One pointed out that if he were to keep up his slugging pace over the entire season, he would hit 70 homers. Forget it, Mark advised him, the very notion was ridiculous.

> "He had an attitude you'd like to copy and distribute to all young players."
>
> —JIM LEFEBVRE, Oakland coach

Reggie Jackson, in his final season, congratulates Mark after a home run. Mark's 49 homers in 1987 broke Jackson's club record of 47.

The lack of privacy and the pressure to keep hitting home runs wore Mark down. On the road he and his roommate, Terry Steinbach, had to instruct hotel operators not to put calls through to their room. At home, Mark and Kathy felt their relationship straining under the pressure of the home run chase. He was too stubborn to admit to her that he was having problems, and she was not experienced enough to draw him out. The fact that she was pregnant with their first child—and the due date coincided with the end of the season—only made things more tense. Mark finished the year with 49 home runs to lead the major leagues. He had a chance to hit 50, but took the last game off so he could be with Kathy while she delivered their son, Matthew.

> "Just because I'm an athlete doesn't mean I'm immune to problems. I had problems like anybody else."
>
> —MARK MCGWIRE

The following season, Mark learned something disturbing about being a major leaguer: having one great season only increases the pressure to produce another. And it also increases the determination of great season only increases the pressure to produce another. And it also increases the determination of

Mark McGwire 1B

Mark's 1988 baseball cards were in high demand despite of an "off" season.

pitchers to keep you from beating them. Indeed, throughout the 1988 season, Mark rarely saw more than one or two decent pitches a game.

Although he turned in another excellent performance (32 home runs and 99 RBIs), Mark felt like a failure. It hardly mattered to him that the rest of the A's were benefiting from his presence in the Oakland lineup, or that the team was more than 10 games in front of the defending champion Minnesota Twins. Or that the A's were favored to win the World Series. Mark was still miserable.

Kathy was miserable, too. Right before the series, she took Matthew —who had just turned one—and left Mark.

Mark had a lot on his mind as he prepared to play in the 1988 World Series. The A's lost in five games to the Los Angeles Dodgers, as Mark batted just .059.

"I can remember lying in bed in the middle of the night and Mark saying, 'I can't hit the baseball anymore. I'm done. I've lost it. I've got to quit.'"

KATHY McGWIRE

Trade *Bait*

In Sammy Sosa's first game with the Texas Rangers, he rapped out a single and a double against New York in Yankee Stadium, also known as the "House that Ruth Built." It was an impressive debut, but hardly one to suggest that he would one day outhomer the mighty Babe. Indeed, a month later, the Rangers sent Sammy down to Class-AAA Oklahoma City. The team felt he was not mature enough to hold his own in the heat of a pennant race, and Texas desperately needed someone who had been through it all before.

The Rangers started talking to the Chicago White Sox, who were languishing in last place. Texas wanted thirty-year-old Harold Baines, one of the best RBI men in baseball. The Rangers offered veteran second baseman Scott Fletcher, along with a prospect. The Sox countered by asking for

Sammy had an impressive debut with the Texas Rangers.

two prospects: pitcher Wilson Alvarez and Sammy. In a move they would long regret, the Rangers agreed to the trade. Sammy finished the 1989 season as Chicago's regular rightfielder, then nailed down the starting job the following spring.

The winter after his rookie year, Sammy went home to San Pedro to relax and enjoy life as the town's newest celebrity. One night, he spotted a familiar face at a local nightclub—a woman he had seen dancing on a favorite television show. Sammy scribbled out a note and asked a waiter to bring it to her. It read, If you will do me the honor of having one dance with me, it will be the start of a beautiful relationship. The woman's name was Sonia. She saved Sammy a dance, and the following year they were married.

The White Sox believed that Sammy could be a dominant player, but could not wait for him to develop.

Considering his inexperience, Sammy's 1990 campaign was superb. Still playing primarily on instinct, he took the league by surprise, swiping 32 bases, gunning down 14 runners, and becoming the only player in the American League to reach double figures in doubles, triples, and homers. Were it not for Mark McGwire and the mighty Oakland A's, Chicago would have made the playoffs. In fact, only the A's and Pirates had better records in all of baseball.

Coming off such a promising season, Sammy was projected to be a player who would soon join the "30–30 club" (30 steals and 30 home

"Sammy didn't believe there were any base hits in right field."

—BILLY WILLIAMS

runs in the same year). On Opening Day of the 1991 season, he smashed a pair of home runs, raising expectations even higher. But as the year wore on, he fell apart at the plate, batting just .203.

Sammy was learning that making it to the majors was a lot easier than staying in the majors. The pitchers had discovered his weaknesses, and he was unable to adjust. They pitched him away, yet he insisted on trying to pull everything to left field. Realizing that he liked to hit fastballs early in the count, pitchers started him off with curves, sliders, and sinkers. Sammy would either pound these deliveries into the ground or miss them completely. Then, when he was looking for more off-speed stuff, they would blow fastballs past him.

Part of the trouble went back to never having had any coaching as a kid; his fundamentals were still shaky. Another contributing factor was Sammy's belief that his natural talent would ultimately win out. He was not overestimating his own abilities, but he *was* underestimating his competition.

That winter the White Sox went shopping for a power hitter who could join sluggers Frank Thomas and Robin Ventura in the middle of the lineup. Their crosstown rivals, the Chicago Cubs, offered George Bell. They wanted Sammy in return. The Sox *had* to make the deal; there was no guarantee that Sammy would develop into a middle-of-the-lineup player in 1992, and the team wanted to finish first in the Western Division. The deal was done just before Opening Day.

Sammy surveys his new home, the friendly confines of Wrigley Field.

Ups & Downs
& *Other Stuff*

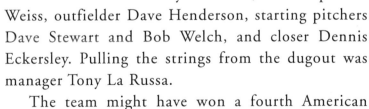

Over the 1989 and 1990 seasons, Mark was able to combat the sadness of his broken marriage by immersing himself in baseball. He continued to put up great numbers, and the Oakland A's reached the World Series twice more. He and Jose Canseco combined to give the team the most potent one-two punch in the game. From 1987 to 1990, they combined to hit 280 homers and drive in 815 runs, earning the nickname "Bash Brothers." The supporting cast was a good one. It included third baseman Carney Lansford, shortstop Walt

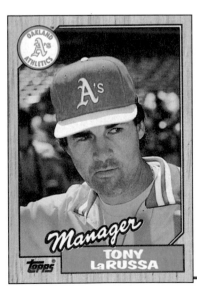

Weiss, outfielder Dave Henderson, starting pitchers Dave Stewart and Bob Welch, and closer Dennis Eckersley. Pulling the strings from the dugout was manager Tony La Russa.

The team might have won a fourth American League pennant in 1991 had Mark not bottomed out. He felt depressed prior to the season, and neglected his training. During the year, he lost his drive to stay ahead of the pitchers. The result was a batting average so low that Mark begged out of the season's final games for fear that it might drop below

Tony La Russa's Topps baseball card from 1987, his first full year as manager of the Oakland A's.

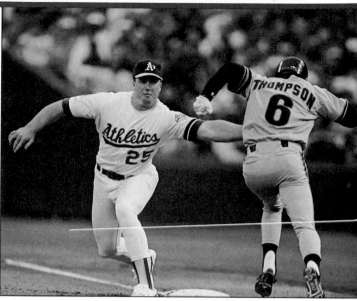

Mark helped the A's sweep the San Francisco Giants in four games in the 1989 World Series. Before the start of Game 1, he shares a laugh with former Olympic teammate Will Clark (top, left). Mark stretches for an errant throw during Game 1 of the 1989 World Series (top, right). Mark celebrates the final out of his first World Series championship (bottom, left).

*Mark tries to pick off Lance Johnson of the White Sox during a 1990 game.
Mark won the Gold Glove for fielding excellence that year.*

.200. That was the last straw. After the season, he made himself make a choice: either quit baseball, or rededicate himself to the game.

That winter, he turned to his youngest brother, J.J., for help. His promising sports career had ended with an eye injury at the age of fifteen, but he had since become a personal trainer. J.J. put Mark through a killer training program designed to pump up the muscles he used most. Meanwhile, Mark sought professional counseling to work out his emotional problems. When the 1992 season got started, Mark began

"People have no idea the hard work that goes on behind the scenes to be successful and stay at a certain level year in and year out. It's the toughest thing to do."

—MARK MCGWIRE

crushing the ball. He blasted 42 home runs, had the league's highest slugging percentage, and helped the A's return to the top of the American League's Western Division.

Unfortunately, Mark's next two seasons were marred by back and heel injuries that kept him out of all but 74 games. The old Mark would have gotten angry and frustrated—and maybe even quit. The new Mark decided to make the best of the situation and learn how to become a more complete hitter. For two seasons, he studied pitchers and experimented with different swings. When he returned to the lineup in 1995, he was awesome. The big difference in Mark was that he had become very selective at the plate—he

no longer got himself out by swinging at poor pitches. If a hurler wanted to get him out, he had to throw Mark a strike. Otherwise, he would be satisfied with a walk. He also shortened his swing, giving him a split second more to judge pitches.

By 1996 word had spread among pitchers that you had to give Mark McGwire something decent to hit. Those who fell behind in the count and chose to lay one over paid the price, as Mark walloped 52 home runs and recorded one of the highest slugging averages in major league history. Those who refused to give in watched helplessly as he trotted to first base with a career-high 116 walks.

Mark gets a broken-bat single in a 1995 game. His new compact stroke enabled him to fight off pitches he once popped up or missed altogether.

Mark exhibits perfect home run form in a 1997 game against the Texas Rangers. This ball left the park for a grand slam.

In 1997 the home run barrage continued, as Mark amassed 31 by the All-Star break. For the second time in his career, "McGwire Mania" erupted. After every game his locker was swarming with reporters asking if he could hit 61, and trying to stir up a rivalry with Ken Griffey, Jr., who was matching him homer for homer. This time, Mark knew how to handle the circus. He was gracious, modest, and relaxed.

As great a hitter as Mark had become, he was not fitting into the 1997 plans of the Oakland A's. The team was rebuilding with young, inexpensive players and their superstar first baseman was too old and making too much money. At the end of July, the St. Louis Cardinals, who were desperate for power, traded three young pitchers to the A's in return for Mark. He was due to be a free agent at season's end, so in effect the Cards were merely "renting" him for two months.

> "Things happen for a reason. Hard work pays off."
> —MARK McGWIRE

But what a two months it was! Mark slammed 24 homers in 51 games, giving him 58 for the year—the most of anyone in the majors. It also was the first time anyone had ever totaled 20 or more round-trippers for two different teams in the same season.

St. Louis management, fearful of how the fans might react if Mark was allowed to sign with another team, asked him what kind of contract would make him stay. To their surprise, he asked for a third less than he could have gotten on the open market. Mark loved St. Louis, and appreciated the way the fans had treated him during his short time there. He preferred to stay put.

At a news conference announcing the deal, Mark told the press that he would earmark $1 million a year to fund a foundation he was creating to help abused children. The more he spoke about the charity, the more emotional he became. By the end of the press conference, the man who once allowed his marriage to disintegrate because he was afraid to show his emotions was crying like a baby. "I've run into reporters, news people and just people on the street who wouldn't talk to anyone

> "He shoots for the back row. The rest of us shoot for the front row."
> —STEVE FINLEY, All-Star Outfielder

about what happened in their childhood, but for some reason they told me," Mark says of his involvement in this important cause. "When you have a child of your own, you definitely look at things differently."

Mark still is not sure what was going through him, but after that day he felt as if the weight of the world had been lifted from his shoulders. He could hardly wait for the 1998 season to begin.

Crosstown
Clubber

Sammy Sosa's Cub career started slowly, thanks to a succession of injuries during the 1992 season. In 1993, he had his best year as a major leaguer, becoming the 14th major leaguer (and first Cub) to hit 30 homers and steal 30 bases in the same season. In 1994, he was on pace for another excellent campaign when a labor dispute ended the season after just 105 games. Sammy was now the hottest topic in the Windy City. Clearly, the Cubs had gotten a steal. But what exactly did they have?

In terms of age, Sammy was entering his prime baseball years. But in baseball terms, he was just a kid. For instance, Sammy still did not know how to "work" an at bat to get the pitch he wanted. He often played hitters incorrectly in the outfield, and made frequent base-running mistakes.

Sammy's first card as a Chicago Cub was issued by Leaf in 1992.

SAMMY SOSA CF

Team leader Mark Grace saw Sammy's potential the first day he joined the Cubs, but could not believe how undisciplined he was at the plate. "He was a real rockhead," Grace recalls.

Furthermore, many of the game's nuances—such as hitting behind runners and throwing to the cutoff man—were completely alien to him. Some fans claimed these things as evidence that he was not a team player.

Sammy heard the criticism and battled it the only way he could. He worked hard to catch up on the fundamentals, and slowly began to learn the game. Ironically, it was his teammates who got most upset at charges that he was not a team player. They knew otherwise. Sammy's goals went beyond just being a solid ball player. He wanted to be the best player the town had ever seen. Slowly but surely, the rough edges came off Sammy's game. In 1995 he hit 36 home runs and topped the 100-RBI mark for the first time. In 1996 he finished with 40 round-trippers and 100 RBIs despite missing the final six weeks of the season.

Believing Sammy was ready to fulfill his promise, the Cubs rewarded him with a $42 million contract extension during the 1997 season. Yet instead of taking a big step forward, he took a giant step backward. His average plummeted to its lowest level in six years, his on-base percentage was among the poorest in all of baseball, he struck out a league-high 174 times, and of his 119 RBIs only a handful came when the team really needed them. The low point of the season came when manager Jim

Sammy had a tough year after signing a huge contract.

Riggleman lost his patience and chastised Sammy in the dugout before a national television audience.

Cub fans felt betrayed. They loved Sammy. How could he "take the money and run"?

Of course, that was hardly the case. After Sammy signed his multimillion-dollar contract, he started the Sammy Sosa Charitable Foundation, which raises money for needy children. "This foundation is my opportunity to give kids in need a chance at a better life," he says. "I was lucky enough to get the chance to play baseball. I want to give less fortunate kids the help they need."

Not that he had been stingy in the past. On the contrary, Sammy might be baseball's most generous superstar. After his 30-30 season in 1993, Sammy financed construction of the 30-30 Plaza, a complex of retail stores and offices in the Dominican Republic. Two of his sisters own businesses in the mall (a boutique and hair salon). In the middle of the plaza is the Fountain of Shoeshine Boys, which features a statue of Sammy. All coins tossed into the fountain go to the shoeshine boys of San Pedro.

Come December, the Sammy Claus World Tour will take to the road again. Sammy loves to play the role of St. Nick, visiting hospitals both in the U.S. and Dominican Republic. The giving does not stop after the holidays, however. Any time an idea pops into Sammy's head, he is willing to whip out his checkbook. After he bought his oldest daughter, Keisha, her

> "There was too much pressure...pressure from the contract, pressure to do it all. I felt if I didn't hit a home run, we wouldn't win. I was trying to hit two home runs in one at bat."
>
> —SAMMY SOSA

own computer—and saw how much she was learning—he discovered that none of the public schools in the Dominican Republic had computers. So Sammy purchased 250 units and shipped them to his homeland, with instructions that they be put in the classrooms. When he found out his hometown of San Pedro did not have a modern ambulance, he bought one and sent it down. "I'll never forget where I came from," Sammy says. "These are my people. I'm proud of the United States—it's given me everything I have—gave me the opportunity to be Sammy Sosa. But I have to remember these are my people, people I have to take care of, people I have to give jobs to. This is my life."

Sammy's generosity of time and money earned him the cover spot in BASEBALL WEEKLY's feature on players and teams that give back to their communities.

Mac
Attack

On the afternoon of March 31, 1998, Mark McGwire settled into the batter's box for his third plate appearance of what many predicted would be a historic season. The first three Cardinals in the inning had reached base against Los Angeles Dodger starter Ramon Martinez, who peered into catcher Mike Piazza for the signal. After taking a pitch for ball one, Mark crushed Martinez's next delivery over the left field fence to become only the 21st player in history to hit a grand slam on Opening Day. Mark followed with three more homers over the next three games; ten days later, he hit three in one game against the Arizona Diamondbacks. By the end of April, he had 11 home runs.

Mark's 16th home run of the season came against Livan Hernandez of the Florida Marlins. The ball traveled 545 feet to dead center field, making it the longest ever hit at Busch Stadium, and the longest of Mark's career. A three-homer game against the Phillies on May 19 brought Mark's tally to 20 homers. He had 27 by the end of the month, with 17 coming at home. No one had ever hit more that 17 homers at Busch in an entire *season*, and Mark still had four months to go!

JOHNNY MIZE
FIRST BASEMAN

Johnny Mize belted 43 homers for the Cardinals in 1940. His cards are among the most collectible of any St. Louis player.

By June, the race for the record was officially on. Every day, baseball fans could find a chart in the newspaper comparing Mark's torrid home run pace to those of Roger Maris and Babe Ruth during the years they hit 61 and 60, respectively. Every day, reporters crowded around Mark's locker asking the same dreary questions over and over again. Having been through this twice before, Mark knew just how to handle it. He talked with great respect about the legends he was chasing; he answered questions with great candor and sincerity; and he gave lots of credit to his teammates. In years past, fans often rooted against sluggers challenging the all-time home run record. But Mark came off as such a nice guy, everyone in baseball seemed to be pulling for him to do it.

Mark clouted 8 more home runs in July to give him 45; his 44th broke the team record set by Hall of Famer Johnny Mize fifty eight years earlier. After the All-Star Game, Mark decided he would limit the distractions by no longer reading the sports section or watching highlight shows on TV. He also stopped opening his fan mail, which was coming in by the bagful every day.

In August, traditionally Mark's least productive month, his production soared. He belted 10 more home runs, which put him within striking distance of Roger Maris's record. The big news that month, however, concerned Mark's use

Hall of Famer Stan Musial literally "wrote the book" on hitting. "I've never seen such a commotion for a baseball player in this town," he said of fan response to Mark's 1998 season.

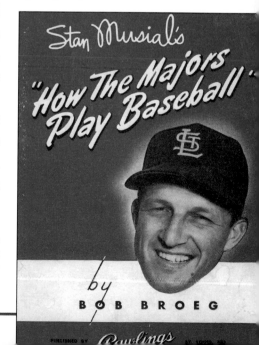

Stan Musial's "How The Majors Play Baseball"

by

BOB BROEG

Mark's
BIO FILE

BORN	October 1, 1963
HEIGHT	6' 5"
WEIGHT	250 lbs.
BATS	Right
THROWS	Right

FAMILY:

Mark did not remarry after his divorce, but lives just a few minutes away from Matthew, Kathy, and her new husband, in Orange County, California. Matthew's birthday is just three days before Mark's, so when the baseball season is over they take a special birthday vacation together.

HOBBY:

Mark likes to spend his free evenings at home watching historical documentaries and science shows on television. His favorite channel-surfing stop is The Learning Channel.

TROPHY CASE:

Mark gives his stuff away to friends, family, and charities, or keeps it in storage. He says there is nothing related to baseball in his house.

HOW'S HIS GOLF GAME:

Mark is now a 10 handicap golfer, which means his game is about one shot per hole shy of professional caliber. In 1993 he and pro golfer Billy Andrade finished second at the prestigious Pebble Beach Pro-Am Tournament. Not surprisingly, Mark can hit the ball as far as anyone on the PGA Tour, including Tiger Woods.

of a muscle-building supplement called androstenedione. The drug is legal and used by athletes in a number of sports, and can be purchased by anyone in a nutrition shop. Mark, who defended his use of "andro," was surprised at all the fuss. If androstenedione is ever proved unsafe or banned by Major League Baseball, Mark said he would simply stop using it. How big a boost did it give him? He could not say. But certainly it was not as great an advantage as, say, the endless hours he has spent watching videotapes of rival pitchers, or practicing his swing in the batting cage.

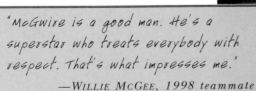

"McGwire is a good man. He's a superstar who treats everybody with respect. That's what impresses me."
—WILLIE McGEE, 1998 teammate

Mark watches another home run leave the park at Busch Stadium in St. Louis.

Slammin'
Sammy

While Mark McGwire was getting the 1998 season off to a bang, Sammy Sosa hardly rated a headline. Sammy launched a respectable 6 homers in April and another 7 in May, but that still gave him less than half of Mark's amazing total. Sammy was more concerned with putting the finishing touches on some important adjustments he made over the winter. After watching tapes of himself and other top hitters, he noticed that he had been rushing his swing, which made him susceptible to off-speed offerings and pitches that darted away from the plate.

To correct this flaw, Sammy actually started his swing later. To gain back the time he "lost" while waiting, he concentrated on recognizing what type of pitch was coming as soon as it left the pitcher's hand. He also altered his stance, bringing the

Sammy signs autographs during spring training.

Sammy beats the throw to second for one of his 18 stolen bases on 1998. He had more combined homers and steals than anyone in the National League.

bat down from above his head so he could get into his swing sooner. These adjustments did not always translate into base hits, but because Sammy was laying off balls he used to swing at, opponents were now forced to give him better pitches to hit. In other words, he was making the same changes to his approach that Mark had a few years earlier.

Finally, in June, it all came together for Sammy, and balls started flying out of the yard. He hit 7 home runs in the first eight days of the month, then blasted 3 in a June 15 game against Cal Eldred of the Milwaukee Brewers. Sammy added 4 more against the Phillies on June 19 and 20 to bring his total for June to 17. His next round-tripper tied the all-time record for homers in a month, set by Rudy York of the Tigers in 1937. It seemed only fitting that this blast—and the record breaker he hit the following day—came against Detroit, in Tiger Stadium. Five days later, Sammy slammed his 20th of the month to extend his own mark. Heading into July, he had 33 homers, just four behind Mark.

Sammy's name was now appearing in those daily home run "progress reports." Sammy felt uncomfortable seeing his name alongside those of Ruth and Maris, but the fans at Wrigley Field had no problem with it. They would chant *MVP! MVP! MVP!* whenever Sammy sprinted out to his position in right field. He would respond by forming a peace sign, kissing his fingers and pounding his chest to say, "Thanks, I love you." Meanwhile, he kept pace with Mark, hitting 9 homers in July—including his first career grand slam. Incredibly, Sammy had gone 4,429 career at bats before hitting one with the bases juiced; the following day, he hit another one!

For a brief moment on August 19, Sammy actually took the lead in the National League home run race. With the Cardinals visiting Chicago, Sammy Sosa slammed number 48. In the same game, however, McGwire hit numbers 48 and 49. Sammy tallied 13 home runs in August to McGwire's 10, giving each 55 heading into the season's final month.

Sammy watches his home run against the Pittsburgh Pirates starter Jason Schmidt Friday, Sept. 4, 1998, in Pittsburgh. The blast was Sosa's 57th of the season.

Sammy enjoys a light moment with fellow 1998 All Stars Derek Jeter (center), Alex Rodriguez (number 3), and Barry Bonds.

Sammy's
BIO FILE

BORN	November 12, 1968	HEIGHT	6'
WEIGHT	200 lbs.	BATS	Right
THROWS	Right		

FAMILY:
Sammy and his wife, Sonia, have four children: Keisha, Kenia, Sammy, Jr., and Michael. Each winter he plays 'Father Christmas' to countless Dominican children, earning him the nickname 'Sammy Claus.'

HOBBY:
Sammy has developed a passion for automobiles. His garage currently houses a Rolls Royce, Ferrari, Viper, Navigator, Expedition, and two Mercedes.

TROPHY CASE:
Next to Sammy's 1998 MVP Award are his three 'treasures': a plaque from fans in the Dominican Republic commemorating the record 20 home runs he hit in June '98, an award from the Cubs for his service to the Chicago community, and a sign that reads "My house is small, no mansion for a millionaire. But there is room for love and there is room for friends."

HOW'S HIS GOLF GAME:
Not too good. Sammy tried the game once and reports, "I hit everything foul: I hit over trees, over houses, over everything."

A September
To Remember

With a new home run record now a virtual certainty, the baseball world sat back and just enjoyed the ride. These guys were a pleasure to watch, both on and off the field. The more that was revealed about them, the more intriguing the home run race became. Fans could not help noticing that, as different as Mark and Sammy first seemed, they actually had much in common. Each had begun his career with great promise, only to have the game overwhelm him. And, ultimately, each found the path to redemption. Now the two were neck and neck in pursuit of history.

It was interesting to watch the two men deal with the crush of media. Mark had almost gotten used to the craziness, and did a great job maintaining an even keel. Sammy, a newcomer to national attention, seemed to thrive on the energy. Both players were feeling the pressure, of course, but they managed to maintain their perspective and sense of humor at the press conferences that followed each home run. Mark

> *"I'll admit it. I get goose pimples,"*
> —TONY LA RUSSA, *Cardinals manager*

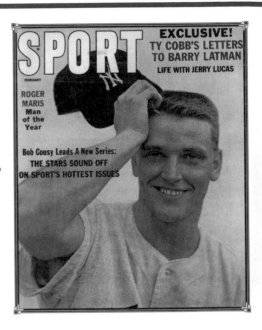

Like Mark, Babe Ruth (left) began his career as a pitcher. When Roger Maris (right) broke the Babe's record, he landed on the cover of SPORT magazine.

and Sammy eventually struck up a friendship, which Mark later said helped keep him loose.

The first target for Mark and Sammy was 60 homers, the number Babe Ruth had hit in 1927. Mark was the first to reach 60, with a two-run blast against the Reds in the season's 142nd game. Two days later, on September 7, Mark hit his 61st homer to tie

> *"I really believe he's up there watching."*
> —MARK MCGWIRE on Babe Ruth

Maris. It came in St. Louis, against Mike Morgan of the Cubs. Standing in right field that day was Sammy, "stuck" on homer number 58. He saluted Mark, who was congratulated by the Maris family after circling the bases.

Number 62—the "big one"—came the next evening off of Steve Trachsel. Mark was so ecstatic that he missed first base, and had to go

> *"My life is kind of like a miracle."*
> —SAMMY SOSA

back and touch the bag. Waiting for him at home plate were his jubilant teammates, as well as the Cardinals' new bat boy: Matthew McGwire. Mark's son had flown in from California to be with him when he broke the record. Matthew had so much fun that he stayed until the end of the season.

Mark watches his 61st home run of the season. The homer tied Roger Maris's 37-year-old major league record.

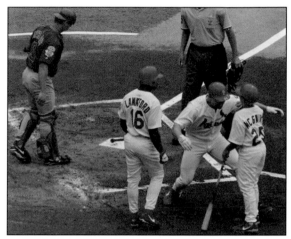

After crossing the plate, Mark grabs his son, Matthew, as teammate Ray Lankford looks on.

Happy birthday, Dad! Mark hugs his parents after hitting number 61. John McGwire (right) turned 61 the same day.

Mark may have been baseball's new single-season home run record holder, yet by no means was the season finished. Indeed, there was a very real possibility that he might finish the year *without* the record. There were still 17 games left to be played, and Sammy was only 4 homers behind.

Mark watches his record-breaking 62nd home run—a line drive to left that just cleared the fence. Pitcher Steve Trachsel (right) watches helplessly as he becomes a part of history.

Mark hugs family members of the late Roger Maris after breaking their father's major league single-season home run record (above).

Sammy, who was in right field for the Cubs, embraces Mark.

Now it was the Chicago star's turn to get hot. Sammy blasted number 60 on September 12 and numbers 61 and 62 on September 13 to pull even with Mark. Mark

> "What a way to give something back to the fans of St. Louis for the way they've treated me since coming over here—to get number 62 at home."
>
> —MARK MCGWIRE

responded with his 63rd homer of the year on September 15, but Sammy matched him a day later. Mark reached 65 with two more round-trippers over the next five days, while Sammy did not hit any. On September 23, however, Sammy hit a pair of home runs against the Brewers to tie Mark at 65, then hit another on September 25 to pull ahead, with 66. Sammy had the lead for all of 45 minutes. In St. Louis, Mark hit his 66th against the Expos.

Heading into the season's last weekend, fans wondered who would emerge as the winner in this thrilling long-distance duel. With the Cubs still in the hunt

Sammy hops in the air as he watches his 62nd home run of the season leave the ball park. He and Mark were tied at 62 for three days.

Sammy rips home run number 63—a grand slam off Brian Boehringer of the Padres. Sammy had never hit a bases-loaded homer prior to 1998.

for the playoffs, Sammy would have to do more situational hitting, so there might be times when it would be imprudent to try for a home run. In St. Louis, the focus would be completely on Mark— he would be attempting to hit every ball over the fence, while the pitchers would be trying to keep him in the ballpark.

In a final, unforgettable flurry, Mark pulled ahead for good, clubbing two homers on Saturday and two more on Sunday to finish with 70!

Sammy's son, Sammy, Jr., applauds as his dad receives the Commissioner's Historic Achievement Award from Baseball Commissioner Bud Selig during Sammy Sosa Day festivities at Wrigley Field on September 20, 1998.

Aftermath

After 162 games, the Cubs found themselves tied with the Giants for the wild-card spot for the playoffs, meaning the two teams would have to meet in a winner-take-all game to determine who would continue on. Technically, this contest was part of the regular season, so Sammy still had a chance to add to his total and

> "Only now is Sammy at a mature stage. Only now is he becoming the player he always could have been."
>
> —OMAR MINAYA, scout

maybe even tie Mark. Several players have hit four home runs in a game, although never in a game as big as this.

In the playoff against the Giants, San Francisco pitchers refused to give Sammy anything he could drive. In past years, he might have tried for home runs anyway, but the 1998 version of Sammy Sosa was satisfied to take what opponents gave him. He singled twice and scored two runs in Chicago's 5–3 victory. Against the Braves in the divisional series, Sammy and the Cubs did not

> "McGwire's a monster. He's got Nintendo numbers!"
>
> —GREG VAUGHN, All-Star outfielder

> *"So where do I go from here? My next big career goal is to hit 500 home runs."*
>
> —MARK MCGWIRE

> *"My next goal would be to go to Heaven."*
>
> —SAMMY SOSA

fare well. Atlanta's great starters shut down the Cubs' offense, and swept them out of the postseason in three straight.

The final numbers on Mark and Sammy are still hard to believe. Mark's 70 homers were accompanied by a .299 batting average and 147 RBIs—excellent stats by any measure, but particularly good considering pitchers were extra careful not to give him anything good to hit. When he did swing, Mark was murderous. Of every five balls he was able to put into play during 1998, one was a home run. His .752 slugging percentage was the highest in seventy-one years, and his 162 bases on balls set an all-time league record. Sammy's 134 runs scored were the most in baseball in 1998, and the most by a Cub since 1929. Sammy's 66 home runs generated 158 RBIs, the most by a major leaguer since 1949—and one more than his old buddy, Juan Gonzalez, had for the Rangers over in the American League. After the season, Juan was honored as the American League MVP, while Sammy was named the National League's MVP.

Sammy greets photographers outside Wrigley Field after he was voted the National League MVP for 1998. He won in a landslide over Mark, getting 30 of 32 first-place votes and 438 points in balloting by the Baseball Writers' Association of America.

Here is where Mark and Sammy ranked in some key offensive categories:

	Mark	Sammy
Home Runs	70 (1st, NL)*	66 (2nd, NL)
RBIs	147 (2nd, NL)	158 (1st, NL)
Game-Winning RBIs	16 (4th, NL)	20 (1st, NL)
Hits	152	198 (5th, NL)
Extra-Base Hits	91 (1st, NL)	86 (3rd, NL)
Runs	130 (2nd, NL)	134 (1st, NL)
Slugging	.752 (1st, NL)	.647 (2nd, NL)
Walks	162 (1st, NL)**	73
Intentional Walks	28 (2nd, NL)	14 (3rd, NL)
On Base Percentage	.470 (1st, NL)	.377

*Major League Record   ** National League Record

Great players and great friends, Sammy and Mark made baseball fun again for millions of fans.

Going, Going, Gone

The breakdown of Mark and Sammy's 136 home runs says a lot about the seasons they had. Thirty-six of Mark's homers either tied the game or put the Cardinals ahead, while Sammy had 27 homers that pulled the Cubs even or put them out in front. The average distance of Mark's blasts was more than 420 feet, with five, 500-footers to his credit. Sammy averaged more than 400 feet per dinger, with one, 500-foot shot. Mark's favorite victims in 1998 were Florida and Chicago, against whom he homered seven times each. Sammy absolutely murdered the Milwaukee Brewers, with 12 round-trippers. The shortest homer hit by either player was 340 feet—a chip shot to the right by Sammy against the Minnesota Twins. Ironically, Mark's least impressive blast was his most famous: the 341-foot line drive against the Cubs that shattered Maris's record.

Sammy's *homers*

12 Left Field

22 Left-Center Field

10 Center Field

11 Right-Center Field

11 Right Field

66

Home: 35   Away: 31

Mark's *homers*

37 Left Field

17 Left-Center Field

13 Center Field

3 Right-Center Field

0 Right Field

70

Home: 38   Away: 32

Thank You, *Guys!*

All numbers aside, the greatest accomplishment for Mark and Sammy in 1998 may have been that they restored America's faith in baseball. After the labor dispute of 1994 led to the cancellation of the World Series, fans stayed away from the ballpark in droves, television ratings plummeted, and—worst of all—a lot of children *stopped* playing baseball. Even as attendance crept back up in recent years, most people had not reinvested much emotion in the game. They had forgiven baseball its sins, but were slow to reopen their hearts.

The 1998 season changed all that, mostly due to these two men. They chased down two of the biggest legends in all of sports with class and dignity, and in the end Mark and Sammy *joined* Roger and the Babe more than they

John Cardinal O'Connor blesses Sammy after presenting him with the Medal of John Paul II at St. Patrick's Cathedral in New York Friday, Oct. 16, 1998. Sammy was recognized for "the great sportsmanship he displayed that inspired our youth."

surpassed them. They also reminded us why baseball is the most American of games. In what other sport could two athletes come together from so far apart—culturally, economically, and geographically—and bring the country so close together?

In a summer of demoralizing economic and political turmoil, Mark McGwire and Sammy Sosa held up a mirror to the people in the United States, and for the first time in a long time, we liked what we saw.

Our home run heroes made baseball fun again.

Mark blows a trademark Sosa kiss to his friend Sammy.

"I have run into fans on the street who said...it's because of what I am doing and Sammy's doing and other great players that the fans are coming back. They're excited about it. All I can say is thank you."

—MARK McGWIRE

Four Things About SAMMY SOSA You Probably Didn't Know

1 Sammy grew up in a two-room apartment in a building that had formerly been a public hospital.

2 When Sammy signed with the Texas Rangers in 1985, there was not a single Hispanic player on the team. By the time he reached the majors, Texas had eight Latinos on the major league roster, including starters Julio Franco (Dominican Republic), Rafael Palmeiro (Cuba), and Ruben Sierra (Puerto Rico).

3 On August 14, 1995, Sammy hit the 10,000th home run in Chicago Cubs history.

4 When hurricane Georges ravaged the Dominican Republic in the fall of 1998, Sammy donated as much time and money as he could to help his fellow Dominicans. After the season ended, he threw himself into the relief effort, raising money in the United States and flying home to help raise the spirits of his country.

Sammy and his wife, Sonia, (left) are cheered in San Pedro de Macoris, Dominican Republic. Sosa's return was called a Day of National Celebration.

Four Things About MARK McGWIRE You Probably Didn't Know

1 Mark's dad was a victim of polio as a child. His participation in sports was primarily limited to golf and cycling.

2 For a few months in high school, Mark wore his hair in an "afro."

3 Mark's brother Dan was a star quarterback for San Diego State University, and was the top choice of the Seattle Seahawks in the 1991 NFL draft.

4 The Cardinals did not make the playoffs in 1998, but Mark still managed to leave his imprint on the World Series. Sitting in the stands during the final game between the Yankees and Padres, he reached over the wall, snagged a foul ball, and received a standing ovation.

*Mark is cheered by thousands of fans after
breaking the record that many thought could never be broken.*

Index